A FIRESIDE BOOK
PUBLISHED BY SIMON & SCHUSTER INC.
NEW YORK, LONDON, TORONTO, SYDNEY, TOKYO

Most of these cartoons previously appeared in *All New Zap Comix, Cavalier, East Village Other, Help!, Yarrowstalks,* and *Underground Review.*

First FIRESIDE EDITION, June 1988

Published by Simon & Schuster Inc.
Simon & Schuster Building
Rockefeller Center
1230 Avenue of the Americas
New York, NY 10020

Published by arrangement with the author

Published in 1968 as a William Cole Book

Fireside and colophon are registered trademarks
of Simon & Schuster Inc.
Manufactured in the United States of America

10 9 8 7 6 5 4 3 2 1

Library of Congress Cataloging in Publication Data

Crumb, R.
    R. Crumb's head comix.

    "A Fireside book."
    Reprint. Originally published: New York: Viking
Press, 1968.
    1. American wit and humor, Pictorial. I. Title.
II. Title: Head comix.
NC1429.C83A4   1988   741.5'973   88-3608

ISBN 0-671-66153-1

CONTENTS

TWENTY YEARS LATER...

BY THE 'HEAD' HIMSELF, R. CRUMB

AH, TO BE TWENTY-FOUR YEARS OLD IN THE YEAR 1967!! WHAT VISTAS!! WHAT POSSIBILITIES!! WHAT GRAND EXCITEMENTS! STONED-OUT DIZZINESS!! EUPHORIA! THEN THERE WAS ALSO "THE HORROR! THE HORROR!" LIFE WAS ANYTHING BUT DULL ON THE WORST OF DAYS IN THE YEAR 1967...BUM TRIPS, BAD SCENES..."THAT'S COOL TOO!"

EVEN WHEN SADDLED WITH A WIFE WHOSE ONLY WISH WAS FOR A NICE HOUSE IN THE SUBURBS, A COUPLE OF KIDS AND A HUBBY WITH STEADY INCOME. SHE WOULD'VE BEEN JUST AS HAPPY IF WE'D STAYED IN CLEVELAND, TAKEN THAT HOUSE IN GARFIELD HEIGHTS, AND I'D KEPT MY POSITION WITH THE GREETING CARD COMPANY, STEADILY GETTING RAISES AND PROMOTIONS. BUT NO, I HAD TO DRAG HER ALL OVER HELL AND CREATION, PLOP HER DOWN RIGHT IN THE MIDDLE OF THE VORTEX OF CRAZINESS, THE HAIGHT-ASHBURY OF EARLY 1967. "WHEN ARE YOU GOING TO GROW UP AND ACCEPT YOUR RESPONSIBILITIES," SHE USED TO SCOLD ME... "GROWING UP" WAS THE FURTHEST THING FROM MY MIND, BUT STILL I FELT GUILTY. "SHE'S RIGHT...I'M IMMATURE, I'M ALL MIXED UP," IS HOW I'D THINK ABOUT IT...."JUST WANNA HAVE FUN IN THE WORST WAY... FUCK AROUND...GO OFF AND BE A HIPPY, FREE OF CARES AND WORRIES...NO JOB, NO MONEY, NO STUFF, EXCEPT MY SKETCHBOOK AND MY SILLY BANJO-UKE." I'D RUN OFF WITH MY PALS AND GET HIGH IN THE WOODS, COME BACK HOME TAIL BETWEEN MY LEGS. SHE'S SITTING IN THE MIDDLE OF THE BED LIKE AN INDIAN SQUAW READING *FAMILY CIRCLE*. WE LIVED ON WELFARE. IT WAS EASY. NOBODY EVER THOUGHT ABOUT THE FUTURE EXCEPT IN SOME VAGUE PHILOSOPHIC SENSE.

WE'D FOUND A WAY OUT, OUR GENERATION...BEFORE THIS NEW HIPPY THING, THERE WEREN'T TOO MANY WAYS TO DODGE THE STANDARD PATTERN. YOU GOT OUT OF HIGH SCHOOL, YOU WENT TO THE ARMY OR COLLEGE, THEN YOU GOT A JOB, GOT MARRIED, HAD KIDS, WENT INTO DEBT, THAT WAS IT. LOOKING AROUND AT THIS 'GROWN UP' WORLD, IT LOOKED LIKE A MISERABLE HELL TO ME. MY PARENTS, EVERYBODY'S PARENTS...THEY WEREN'T ENJOYING LIFE AT ALL...THEIR NERVES WERE SHOT...THEY FRETTED AND FOUGHT ABOUT MONEY...I WANTED NONE OF IT... I RESOLVED NEVER TO GET MARRIED OR HAVE KIDS. (BEEN MARRIED TWICE—TWO KIDS) I WANTED TO ESCAPE. BUT THERE SEEMED TO BE NO WAY OUT. WHAT WOULD I DO OUT THERE IN THE WORLD? HOW WOULD I LIVE? YIPE!

IN THE EARLY 'SIXTIES I USED TO READ *PLAYBOY* AND BE MILDLY DAZZLED BY THE URBAN SOPHISTICATE LIFE GLORIFIED IN ITS PAGES. I TOYED WITH DREAMS OF MAKING IT BIG AS A COMMERCIAL ARTIST IN NEW YORK. I'D HAVE MY OWN SNAZZY BACHELOR DIGS, TAKE BEAUTIFUL, STYLISH WOMEN OUT TO LITTLE HIP JAZZ CLUBS, AND FUCK 'EM AFTERWARDS BACK AT MY BACHELOR DIGS. I FIGURED I'D CHANGE MY NAME, LEAVE OFF THE LAUGHABLE 'CRUMB' PART, USE MY MIDDLE NAME AS MY LAST NAME, AND SIGN MY WORK

'BOB DENNIS.' LATER ON I DID TRY TO MAKE IT AS A COMMERCIAL ARTIST IN NEW YORK...TRIED FOR NINE MONTHS OF THE HARDEST SLAVE LABOR OF MY LIFE. I WORKED LIKE A DAWG FOR VARIOUS PUBLISHERS AND TOPPS GUM CO. I WASN'T SHARP ENOUGH TO COMPETE IN THE RAT RACE, AND ANYWAY IT WASN'T WORTH IT. I GAVE UP AND SLUNK BACK TO CLEVELAND AND THE CARD COMPANY. ALL THIS WITH THE WIFE IN TOW, MIND YOU..... PLUS I'D ALREADY STARTED TAKING MASSIVE DOSES OF LSD AND KIND OF FORGOT ABOUT THE WHOLE IDEA OF PURSUING A CAREER. LOOKING AT THE HUSTLE AND BUSTLE THROUGH PSYCHEDELICISED EYES IT ALL SEEMED LIKE A COMPLETE SHAM, A PETTY SCRAMBLE FOR POSITION AND PRESTIGE. MY VISION OF LIFE HAD BECOME BIBLICAL, EPIC...I WAS SPEECHLESS, DUMBFOUNDED BY THIS...THIS *NONSENSE!*

THEN ONE COLD DREARY EVENING I WAS SITTING AROUND IN ADELE'S BAR AFTER WORK...THAT JOB AT THE CARD COMPANY WAS DRIVING ME TO DRINK. I WAS PUTTING OFF GOING HOME WHEN IN CAME THESE TWO WACKED-OUT CHARACTERS I KNEW. THESE TWO GUYS, BOTH CERTIFIED LUNATICS, TOLD ME THEY WERE ON THEIR WAY TO SAN FRANCISCO THAT VERY NIGHT. THEY SAID SOMETHING EXCITING WAS HAPPENING OUT THERE... A GATHERING TOGETHER OF PEOPLE OF LIKE MIND...ACID-HEADS, DROP-OUTS, HIPSTERS...IT ALL SOUNDED VERY INVITING TO ME... I ASKED IF THEY MIGHT HAVE ROOM FOR ONE MORE... 'SURE! COME ON ALONG,' THEY SAID. I TOLD ANOTHER FRIEND I WAS WITH TO CALL MY WIFE AND INFORM HER THAT I WENT TO SAN FRANCISCO. NO WAY WAS I GOING TO CONFRONT HER MYSELF. ARE YOU KIDDING? SHE WOULD'VE THROWN A ROYAL SNOT-SLINGING FIT! WAS I AFRAID OF HER? I WAS TERRIFIED OF HER!

IT WAS JANUARY, 1967 WHEN I SET OUT FOR THE NEW MECCA. THINK I HAD ABOUT THREE DOLLARS, THE CLOTHES I WAS WEARING, AND MY RAPIDOGRAPH PEN AND THAT'S ALL. WHAT DID I CARE? I WAS ON THE ROAD! SKIP'S CAR WAS A BROKEN DOWN OLD FIAT WITH NO HEATER. WE CREPT ACCROSS THE FROZEN TUNDRAS OF MIDDLE AMERICA AT 35 MILES AN HOUR. SKIP AND TIM TOOK TURNS DRIVING AND SLEEPING IN THE BACK SEAT WHILE I, THE NON-DRIVER, SPENT THE WHOLE TRIP IN THE CO-PILOT SEAT.

SAN FRANCISCO...I COULDN'T BELIEVE MY EYES... I'D NEVER SEEN SUCH A SWEET LI'L OL' CUP-CAKE TOWN. I'D BEEN IN PHILADELPHIA, CLEVELAND, NEW YORK, CHICAGO, DETROIT...PLACES LIKE THAT. BUT SAN FRANCISCO WAS DIFFERENT TWENTY YEARS AGO, TOO...THERE WERE ONLY TWO OR THREE SKYSCRAPERS DOWNTOWN, THERE WAS VERY LITTLE TRAFFIC ON THE STREETS ANYWHERE IN THE CITY. THE NEIGHBORHOODS WERE FULL OF OLD PEOPLE WHO TOOK THE TROLLEY CARS... RENTS WERE QUITE CHEAP FOR BEAUTIFUL OLD VICTORIAN FLATS AND HOUSES...IT REALLY WAS A CHARMIN' PLACE...IT WAS CLEAN, RELAXED, FRIENDLY AND LIBERAL. MAN, IT WAS NICE THEN. I WAS GLAD TO BE THERE.

AND THERE WAS A SENSE OF URGENCY, OF COSMIC POSSIBILITY IN THE AIR THERE IN 1967... A CERTAIN MAGIC GLOW OR LIGHT ABOUT THE PLACE THAT SEEMED

TO BE SAYING, "THIS IS IT...IT'S NOW OR NEVER."
IT SOUNDS SO CORNY BUT I DON'T KNOW HOW
ELSE TO DESCRIBE IT.

THE THREE OF US CRASHED WITH SOME GUY
THEY KNEW. HE HAD A TINY PLACE IN NORTH
BEACH. AFTER A COUPLE OF DAYS THE GUY WAS
OBVIOUSLY GETTING ANNOYED AT US MOOCHING OFF
HIM, EATING ALL HIS FOOD AND TAKING UP THE
ENTIRE FRONT ROOM IN A TWO-ROOM APART-
MENT. SKIP AND TIM WERE OBLIVIOUS BUT I WAS
HYPER-SENSITIVE TO THE GUY'S SCOWLING LOOKS
AND LOW MUTTERINGS. I CAN'T STAND THE THOUGHT
OF BEING A BURDEN TO ANYONE FOR ONE SECOND,
SO I TOOK OFF...WANDERED OUT INTO THE STREETS.
I NEVER SAW THOSE GUYS AGAIN.

I'D ALREADY CHECKED OUT NORTH-BEACH. I
HUNG AROUND THERE FOR AWHILE, AND THEN DE-
CIDED TO TRY TO FIND THIS OTHER NEIGHBORHOOD
OUR HOST HAD TOLD US ABOUT CALLED HAIGHT-
ASHBURY THAT WAS A NEW HOT AREA FOR THE
HIP ONES. I FOUND IT AND WENT INTO A PLACE
CALLED 'THE PSYCHEDELIC SHOP.' A WRITTEN STATE-
MENT ON THE DOOR PROCLAIMED THAT THE INFLU-
ENCE OF PSYCHEDELIC DRUGS ON OUR GENERATION
WAS THE MOST IMPORTANT EVENT SO FAR IN THE
EVOLUTION OF LIFE ON THIS PLANET, ETC; ETC. IN-
SIDE IT WAS CROWDED WITH YOUNG KIDS...THEY
SAT ALONG THE WALL ON ONE SIDE OR MILLED A-
ROUND...THE PLACE REEKED OF INCENSE, MARI-
JUANA AND PATCHOULI OIL. I SAT DOWN AGAINST
THE WALL TOO, WONDERING WHAT TO DO NEXT. I
LOOKED AROUND AT THE PEOPLE; ALL YOUNG, ALL BEAU-
TIFUL, WITH LONG HAIR, LOOSE, FLOWING CLOTHES,
BEADS...THE WHOLE HIPPY LOOK WAS ALREADY IN PLACE
IN THERE...THEY WERE BRIGHT-EYED AND BUSHY-TAILED,
THESE GROOVY KIDS...THIS WAS STILL THE IDEALISTIC
PHASE...WAY BEFORE THE DISILLUSIONMENT, MEDIA
HYPE, DRUG MURDERS...I FELT VERY UNCOMFORTABLE
AND OUT OF PLACE..."HOPE THEY DON'T THINK I'M A
NARC"IS HOW I WAS THINKING. IT MADE ME FEEL
LONELY AND DISCOURAGED. I WAS READY TO GIVE IT
UP AND SLINK ON BACK TO OLD CLEVELAND AGAIN,
AND THE WIFE. I NEVER DID GET TO WHERE I FELT
COMFORTABLE AROUND THOSE FLOWER CHILDREN. THEY
ALWAYS BROUGHT ON INTENSE SELF-CONSCIOUSNESS IN
ME. THEY MADE ME NERVOUS. EVEN THOUGH I WAS
SWEPT UP IN THE GENERAL OPTIMISM AND SHARED A LOT
OF THE SAME LSD-INSPIRED VISIONS AND IDEAS, I NEVER
QUITE GOT WITH THE HIPPY SHTICK. I ALWAYS SEEMED
TO REMAIN AN OUTSIDE OBSERVER OF THESE BAREFOOT
WOOD NYMPHS...GUESS I WASN'T BEAUTIFUL ENOUGH.
I MEAN, IN MY SOUL...DARK DEMONS LURKED IN THERE,
THE HIPPIES COULD TELL...THEY KNEW...THEY PICKED
UP ON YOUR VIBRATIONS....

REMINDS ME OF THIS TIME A PAL OF MINE, A
YOUNG HAPPY-GO-LUCKY HIPPY GUY I KNEW, BROUGHT
THIS GIRL OVER TO MY PLACE. THEY WERE BOTH ON
ACID. THEY CAME IN THE DOOR HIGH AS KITES...
THEY WERE GLOWING...IN A STATE OF GRACE...A COU-
PLE OF SAINTS...LOVE POURED FROM THEIR EYES...
PURE HOLY LOVE... WE SAT AND TALKED QUIETLY...
GRADUALLY THE GIRL BEGAN EYEING ME SUSPICIOUSLY..
PSYCHING ME OUT...SOMETHING ABOUT ME DISTURBED
HER...THE LOVE STOPPED POURING OUT...SHE BEGAN
QUESTIONING ME AS IF I WAS HIDING SOME DARK SE-
CRET. SUDDENLY SHE JUMPED UP AND WALKED
QUICKLY TO THE DOOR... "COME ON, PETE, LET'S GO OUT-
SIDE," SHE SAID URGENTLY. SHE RAN OUT THE DOOR.
PETE LOOKED AT ME, SHRUGGED, AND WENT OUT AFTER
HER. I DON'T KNOW WHAT IT WAS ABOUT ME THAT
BUMMED HER OUT...I GUESS SHE SAW THROUGH THE
BLAND EXTERIOR TO THE SEETHING TURMOIL INSIDE...
SHE SAW THE DEMONS, THAT DID IT. I FELT BAD. I
DIDN'T WANT MY ESSENCE TO CAUSE ANYBODY TO
HAVE A BAD TRIP, BUT YOU CAN'T HIDE ANYTHING
FROM SOMEONE WHO'S HIGH ON LSD.

SO THERE I WAS SITTING ON THE FLOOR OF THE
PSYCHEDELIC SHOP. JUST THEN A GUY I KNEW FROM
CLEVELAND WALKED IN THE DOOR, AND SAW ME. HE
IMMEDIATELY INVITED ME TO STAY AT HIS HOUSE OUT
ON 48TH AVENUE- RIGHT OUT AT THE BEACH. I WAS
SO GREATLY RELIEVED...SUDDENLY EVERYTHING WAS
LOOKING BRIGHTER. AFTER A FEW WEEKS I HAD
SET UP A FREE-LANCE ARRANGEMENT WITH THE GREET-
ING CARD PEOPLE IN CLEVELAND AND HAD MONEY
COMING IN. I RENTED A PLACE ON SACRAMENTO
STREET, AND THEN I MADE MY FIRST MISTAKE. OUT
OF LONELINESS AND GUILT (I SAW HER WEEPING FACE
IN MY DREAMS) I CALLED THE WIFE, BEGGED HER
FORGIVENESS AND ASKED HER TO GET IN THE CAR AND
DRIVE OUT AND JOIN ME. AND SHE DID. THAT WAS
THE END OF ANY POSSIBILITY FOR ME OF PARTICIPAT-
ING IN THE INCREDIBLE FREE-WHEELIN, NEVER-END-
ING ORGY KNOWN AS THE "SUMMER OF LOVE".. GOD,
IT WAS FRUSTRATING...LIVING IN THE MIDDLE OF ALL
THAT AND NOT BEING ABLE TO JOIN IN...NOT EVEN A
LITTLE BIT...NOT EVEN ONE LITTLE TEENY-BOPPER
FLOWER-CHILD FOR BOB.....BOO HOO...15-YEAR-OLD
GIRLS ROAMED THE NEIGHBORHOOD HIGH ON LSD
LOOKING FOR A PLACE TO CRASH...PACKS OF THEM..
FLOCKS OF THEM! IT WASN'T UNTIL A COUPLE OF
YEARS LATER, AFTER I WAS FAMOUS, THAT I STARTED GET-
TING MY FAIR SHARE OF SOME OF THAT HIPPY-CHICK
ACTION. I GUESS I SHOULDN'T GIVE THE IMPRESSION
THAT MY WIFE WAS ENTIRELY TO BLAME...I WAS SUCH
A PAINFULLY SHY WEIRDO...I HAD LOW SELF ESTEEM...I
DIDN'T FIT THE IMAGE OF THE CHRIST-LIKE HIPPY SAINT...
BUT IF I SOUND JUST A TAD BITTER IT'S BECAUSE I AM
...JUST A TAD.

I TRIED TO LOVE THAT WOMAN. I REALLY DID.
BUT I WAS ITCHING FOR ADVENTURE. I WAS COMING
OUT OF MY SKIN. I WAS IN NO MOOD TO BE TIED
DOWN. SHE HAD BEEN THE FIRST WOMAN IN MY
LIFE. I WAS 21 AND SHE ONLY 18 WHEN WE WERE
PUSHED INTO MARRIAGE BY HER PARENTS.

WE'D TAKEN ALOT OF LSD TOGETHER. IT WAS
HARD TO LEAVE HER. I SHOULD KNOW SINCE I LEFT
HER AT LEAST A DOZEN TIMES. ONCE IN THE MID-
DLE OF AN LSD SESSION I BLURTED OUT THAT I WAS
GOING TO LEAVE HER, THAT I WAS TOO YOUNG TO
SETTLE DOWN AND SO FORTH. IT SEEMED LIKE A
REASONABLE ENOUGH ASSERTION TO ME AT THAT
MOMENT. SHE DIDN'T SEE IT THAT WAY. SHE PICKED
UP A BIG DRINKING GLASS AND THREW IT AGAINST
THE WALL HARD, SENDING SHARDS OF GLASS DOWN
ON OUR HEADS IN A SHOWER. SHE GOT UP AND
RAN WEEPING INTO THE BATHROOM. BEHIND THE
LOCKED DOOR SHE SOBBED AND WAILED SOMETHING
ABOUT KILLING HERSELF. OUTSIDE THE DOOR I PLEAD-
ED WITH HER NOT TO DO IT. I WAS STILL PEAKING
ON THE LSD AND HER BEHAVIOR WAS HORRIFYING
TO ME. FINALLY SHE CAME OUT. SHE WAS CALM
AND SEEMED RESIGNED TO MY DECISION TO LEAVE.

I PLANNED TO CLEAR OUT THAT VERY NIGHT,
AND WHILE I PACKED MY SUITCASE SHE HEATED
UP THE CHICKEN SOUP....OUR LAST DINNER TOGETHER,
SHE SAID. WE SAT DOWN TO EAT AND TALKED
CALMLY ABOUT THE WHOLE THING...I TRIED TO AP-
PEASE HER FEARS OF BEING ABANDONED IN THE
WORLD...THE CHICKEN SOUP TASTED STRANGELY
BITTER...SUDDENLY I SPAT IT OUT...I LOOKED AT
HER..."WHAT DID YOU DO TO THIS SOUP?"I DEMAND-
ED...SHE LOOKED FRIGHTENED...I JUMPED UP AND
WENT TOWARDS HER MENACINGLY. "WHAT DID YOU
PUT IN THE SOUP?"I YELLED. SHE BROKE DOWN...
THIRTY SLEEPING PILLS...SHE THOUGHT MAYBE I'D

HAVE A CHANGE OF HEART AFTER A NICE LONG SLEEP. I STARED AT HER IN DISBELIEF, THEN SHOOK MY HEAD AND LAUGHED. "THAT'S IT...YOU ARE REALLY NUTS... I'M LEAVING RIGHT NOW," I SAID. I WENT TO GET MY SUITCASE. THAT'S WHEN SHE PUSHED ME DOWN ON THE COUCH AND SAT ON ME. SHE WAS A HUGE WOMAN, I WAS HELPLESS, I COULDN'T MOVE. SHE HAD ME PINNED. "YOU CAN'T SIT ON ME FOREVER...SOONER OR LATER YOU'LL HAVE TO GET UP," I SAID. SHE SAW THE LOGIC IN THIS AND GOT UP IMMEDIATELY. "I'LL GO," SHE SAID MATTER-OF-FACTLY. "I DON'T WANT TO STAY HERE BY MYSELF. I'M GOING BACK TO CLEVE-LAND." I SAW HER OFF ON A PLANE A COUPLE OF HOURS LATER. THIS HAPPENED IN NEW YORK A YEAR BEFORE I RAN AWAY TO SAN FRANCISCO.

IN THE SUMMER OF 1967, EXACTLY TWENTY YEARS AGO AS I'M WRITING THIS, I RAN AWAY AGAIN, WHILE SHE WAS OUT BUYING GROCERIES. I WAS SITTING A-ROUND FEELING SUFFOCATED, TRAPPED LIKE A CAGED ANIMAL. I GRABBED MY SKETCHBOOK, WALKED DOWN THE STAIRS AND OUT THE FRONT DOOR OF THE BUILDING AND STUCK MY THUMB OUT, RIGHT THERE ON OAK STREET. THAT NIGHT I SLEPT ON A SIDEWALK OUTSIDE OF AUBURN, CALIFORNIA. I WAS HEADING EAST. THE PLAN WAS TO MAKE MY WAY TO CHICAGO AND STAY WITH MY OLD FRIEND MARTY PAHLS. AT DAWN THE NEXT MORNING A KIND OLDER MAN SHOOK ME AWAKE ON MY SIDEWALK AND OFFERED ME A RIDE ABOUT TEN MILES DOWN THE ROAD. NEXT A TRUCK DRIVER TOOK ME AS FAR AS THE TURN-OFF FOR FERNLEY, NEVADA, OUT IN THE DESERT. THERE I STOOD IN THE BLAZING SUN ALL DAY. NOBODY WOULD STOP. IT WAS A SPOT WHERE ALOT OF HITCH HIKERS HAD GOTTEN STRANDED. THERE WAS GARBAGE AND OLD BITS OF BREAD STREWN ON THE GROUND AROUND THE LIGHT-POLE. INSCRIP-TIONS ON THE POLE SAID THINGS LIKE, "GOD HELP ME, I'VE BEEN HERE 21 HOURS," AND "I HATE THIS FUCKING PLACE." EIGHT HOURS PASSED, AND I TOO BEGAN TO HATE THAT FUCKING PLACE AND EVERY SMUG SON-OF-A-BITCH THAT WENT BREEZING BY IN THEIR CAR. THE SUN WAS GO-ING DOWN BEHIND THE DESOLATE HILLS IN THE DISTANCE. I WAS GETTING WORRIED. THEN I SAW A BLESSED SIGHT... AN ABSURD MILK DELIVERY TRUCK PAINTED UP WITH PEACE SYMBOLS AND OTHER SLOPPY PSYCHE-DELIC DESIGNS SLOWLY PUTT-PUTTING DOWN THE HIGH-WAY. I WAS CERTAIN HE'D STOP FOR ME, SO I CAS-UALLY WAVED AS THE MILK TRUCK APPROACHED. AND THEN TO MY AMAZEMENT AND DISMAY HE CRUISED RIGHT ON PAST ME. THIS WAS THE LAST STRAW. I RAN AFTER THE TRUCK, SCREAMING AND WAVING MY ARMS. HE FINALLY SLOWED TO A HALT. I RAN UP AND JUMPED IN THE DOOR BEFORE HE COULD CHANGE HIS MIND. "HOW COME YOU DIDN'T STOP? I WAS DYING OUT THERE," I SAID TO THE DRIVER, A YOUNG HIPPY. HE GRINNED LIKE AN IDIOT AND SAID SOMETHING ABOUT BEING REALLY STONED. "YOU WERE MY LAST HOPE," I SAID. I WENT INTO THE BACK AND FLOPPED DOWN IN THE COZY DEN SOMEONE HAD RIGGED UP BACK THERE...PILLOWS, BLANKETS AND FABRICS ON THE WALLS. I WAS WEAK FROM THAT BLISTERING SUN BEATING ON ME ALL DAY. THERE WERE THREE OTHER YOUNG PEOPLE BACK THERE...A YOUNG GUY WHO WAS DOING HIS "ON THE ROAD" STINT, HITCHING EAST TO BOS-TON. HE WAS A VERY WELL-BRED, EDUCATED, IDEALISTIC YOUNG MAN WHOM I GOT TO KNOW QUITE WELL BEFORE THIS JOURNEY WAS OVER. THE OTHER TWO WERE RUN-AWAY TEEN-AGE GIRLS. WE TALKED FOR A LONG TIME AND SMOKED SOME DOPE. EVENTUALLY THE KID FROM BOSTON GOT INTO AN INTIMATE CLUTCH WITH ONE OF THE GIRLS UNDER THE BLANKETS. THE OTHER GIRL PULLED OUT A BIG HUNTING KNIFE AND SHOWED IT TO ME. "IF ANYBODY TRIES TO MESS WITH ME I'LL STICK THIS THING RIGHT IN THEIR GUT. I KNOW HOW TO USE IT TOO, MAN,

DON'T KID YOURSELF," SHE TOLD ME. I EXPRESSED THE OPINION THAT IT WAS WISE FOR A YOUNG GIRL OUT IN THE WORLD ALONE TO HAVE SOME FORM OF SELF-DEFENSE... THEN I LAY DOWN AND WENT TO SLEEP.

THE NEXT MORNING THE LOCAL COPS IN ROCK SPRINGS, WYOMING PULLED US ALL OUT OF THE VAN. THEY TOOK THE DOPEY DRIVER AND THE TWO RUN-AWAY GIRLS AND PUT THEM IN THE BACK OF THEIR PATROL CAR, AND TOLD ME AND THE OTHER HITCH HIKER TO GET OUT OF TOWN. THEY SAID IF THEY SAW US AROUND TOWN BY SUNDOWN THEY'D PUT US IN JAIL, AND WARNED US THAT HITCH HIKING WAS ILLEGAL IN THE STATE OF WYOMING. NICE FELLAS.

WE WANDERED AROUND THE TOWN, TRYING TO FIG-URE OUT WHAT TO DO. WE CAME TO A RAILROAD YARD AND DISCUSSED HOPPING ON A FREIGHT TRAIN. NEITHER ONE OF US HAD EVER DONE IT BEFORE. WE THOUGHT IT MIGHT BE FUN, NOT TO MENTION THE ONLY WAY OUT OF THERE. WE WAITED AROUND FOR A COUPLE OF HOURS BUT NO TRAINS SEEMED TO BE STARTING EAST. WE GOT TIRED OF WAITING AND WENT BACK INTO TOWN TO GET SOME FOOD SUPPLIES, AND RAN INTO THREE OTHER STRANDED HIPPIES. THESE HIPPIES WERE THE WILD LOW-LIFE TYPE, HIGH ON AMPHETAMINES OR SOMETHING, THEY WERE HYPER AND CRAZY AND SEEMED SLIGHTLY DANGER-OUS... UNPREDICTABLE. MY REFINED TRAVELLING COM-PANION FROM BOSTON DID NOT WISH TO ASSOCIATE WITH THIS ELEMENT. HE TOOK ME ASIDE AND TOLD ME HE THOUGHT THEY WERE TROUBLE. HE WENT OFF TO SEE ABOUT HITCH HIKING OUT OF THE TOWN. THE THREE CRAZ-IES TOLD US THE COPS HAD CHASED THEM OFF THE HIGHWAY AND THREATENED TO BUST THEM FOR HITCH HIKING, JUST AS THEY HAD WITH US. I PUT IN WITH THEM FOR SOME REA-SON. I WAS KIND OF HARE-BRAINED IN THOSE DAYS. THESE THREE, TWO MEN AND A WOMAN, WERE REALLY ASK-ING FOR TROUBLE. THEY'D DO THINGS LIKE RUN INTO A BARBERSHOP, RUN AROUND THE CHAIRS, POKE THE BARBER AND LAUGH AND SHRIEK AND MAKE WISE-CRACKS, RUN OUT OF THERE AND INTO ANOTHER PLACE OF BUSINESS AND DO THE SAME STUFF. THEY ENJOYED FREAKING OUT THE LOCALS, PUTTING THEM THROUGH CHANGES... THE MERRY PRANKSTERS OR SOMETHING... I COULDN'T BELIEVE THEY WERE GETTING AWAY WITH IT. I WAS SURPRISED AT HOW TIMID AND COWED THE TOWNSPEOPLE WERE BY THE SHENANIGANS OF THESE MANIACS. NOBODY DID ANYTHING TO US.... FINALLY THEY STARTED TO WIND DOWN... ROCK SPRINGS WAS SUCH A DRAG, MAN ...THEY WERE GETTING BORED...WE SHUFFLED INTO THE BUS STATION...NO MORE PRANKS... GUESS THEY WERE TIRED OF NOT GETTING ANY REACTION...THEY ALL BOUGHT TICKETS TO SOMEWHERE AND BOARDED A BUS. I HEADED BACK TO THE RAIL-ROAD YARD. IT WAS NIGHT BY THIS TIME. THERE I FOUND MY FRIEND FROM BOSTON, SITTING BY THE TRACKS. I WAS GLAD TO SEE HIM. WE HUNG AROUND THERE AWHILE IN THE BLEAK GLARE OF AN ELECTRIC OVERHEAD LIGHT, BUT NOTHING WAS HAPPENING...NO TRAIN ACTION AT ALL...WE TRUDGED BACK INTO TOWN. IT WAS ONE IN THE MORNING BY NOW. WE WERE PASS-ING THE TOWN SQUARE WHERE A YOUNG COWBOY WAS LOUNGING ON THE GRASS BY THE CANNON. HE RE-SEMBLED MONTGOMERY CLIFT IN "THE MISFITS." HE HAILED US OVER IN A FRIENDLY WAY. WE WENT AND SAT DOWN WITH HIM AND HAD A FUNNY CONVERSA-TION. AFTER AWHILE HE TOLD US THAT WE COULD ALL STAY IN THIS MOTEL NEAR BY WHERE THE OLD LADY NEVER LOCKED THE DOORS OF THE UNUSED ROOMS. IF WE GOT OUT EARLY ENOUGH IN THE MORNING, SHE'D BE NONE THE WISER. HE'D DONE IT BEFORE, NO PROBLEM. IT SOUNDED FABULOUS TO US. WE ALL WENT OVER THERE AND EACH TOOK OUR OWN ROOM. I CRAWLED BETWEEN THOSE SWEET, COOL, CRISP SHEETS AND SLEPT LIKE A BABY.

THE NEXT MORNING, SURE ENOUGH, THE OLD LADY CAUGHT US NAPPING. BEFORE I WAS FULLY AWAKE THE COPS WERE THERE AND HAD ROUNDED US UP. "OKAY,

YOU BOYS ARE GONNA HAVE TO PAY FOR THESE ROOMS OR SUFFER THE CONSEQUENCES," ONE OF THE COPS TOLD US. ME AND BOSTON HAD ABOUT TWO BUCKS BETWEEN US. "I'LL PAY FOR THE ROOMS," THE COWBOY OFFERED. WHAT A DECENT GUY! IT SEEMED HE WAS A LOCAL BOY. THE COPS KNEW HIM BY HIS FIRST NAME. "OKAY, YOU TWO BOYS BETTER GET OUT OF THIS TOWN TODAY," THEY SAID TO US. THE KID FROM BOSTON AND I BEAT IT OUT OF THERE, RELIEVED THAT WE WERE GETTING OFF SO EASILY.

WE SPENT THE DAY SITTING AROUND THE RAILROAD YARD. SOONER OR LATER A TRAIN WOULD COME AND TAKE US AWAY FROM ROCK SPRINGS. WE ATE OUR FOOD SUPPLY AND TALKED. AFTER NIGHTFALL A BIG FREIGHT TRAIN RUMBLED INTO THE YARD. WE WAITED AND SOON IT STARTED UP AGAIN. THIS WAS IT. WE RAN ALONGSIDE OF IT LOOKING FOR A PLACE TO JUMP ON. ALL THE BOXCARS WERE CLOSED UP. IT WAS PICKING UP SPEED RAPIDLY. SOME EMPTY FLAT CARS CAME ALONG, AND WE JUMPED UP ON ONE OF THESE. AS THE TRAIN BEGAN GOING FASTER AND FASTER, THE FLAT CAR STARTED SHAKING VIOLENTLY FROM SIDE TO SIDE. WE HAD TO LIE FLAT ON OUR STOMACHS AND HANG ON TIGHT TO KEEP FROM BEING THROWN OFF. "OH MAN, ARE WE GONNA HAVE TO SPEND THE WHOLE NIGHT LIKE THIS?" I PONDERED. I WAS SCARED. WHAT A COUPLE OF GREENHORN HOBOES WE WERE! AFTER HALF AN HOUR OF THIS ORDEAL THE TRAIN SUDDENLY STOPPED AGAIN. WE WERE IN THE MIDDLE OF NOWHERE... DESERT ALL AROUND. WE HAD TO GET OFF THAT FLAT CAR NO MATTER WHAT. WE JUMPED OFF AND RAN DOWN ALONG THE TRAIN DESPERATELY LOOKING FOR BETTER ACCOMMODATIONS. THE TRAIN STARTED UP AGAIN AS SUDDENLY AS IT HAD STOPPED. "GREAT, WE'RE GONNA BE STRANDED OUT IN THIS DESERT!" I YELLED TO MY COMPANION. JUST THEN WE SPOTTED A FLAT CAR WITH HUGE CULVERT PIPES STACKED ON IT. WE WERE IN LUCK! FRANTICALLY WE GRABBED HOLD AND SCRAMBLED UP ON THE FLATCAR, JUST IN THE NICK OF TIME, AND CRAWLED INTO ONE OF THE HUGE CONCRETE PIPES. IT WAS QUITE COZY COMPARED TO THAT EMPTY FLAT CAR. WE WERE HAPPY AND SOON WE WERE FAST ASLEEP.

THE NEXT AFTERNOON WE GOT OFF THE TRAIN IN CHEYENNE WITH THE INTENTION TO TRY HITCH HIKING AGAIN. WE WERE VERY HUNGRY AND WEARY AS WE LIMPED ALONG INTO THE CITY. WE SAW A RESTAURANT AND WENT IN. WITH OUR LAST FIFTY CENTS, WE STOOD THERE EYEING THE SLICES OF PIE AND DANISHES ON DISPLAY BY THE COUNTER, TRYING TO DECIDE WHICH WAS THE BEST DEAL FOR OUR MONEY. A YOUNG WAITRESS SAW OUR PATHETIC HUNGRY-DOG EXPRESSIONS AND TOLD US TO SIT DOWN, AND SHE BROUGHT US FREE HAMBURGERS! WE GOBBLED THOSE BURGERS UP, THANKED HER AND LEFT THERE BELIEVING THAT THERE WAS STILL SOME BIG HEART OUT THERE IN AMERICA. WE WERE UPLIFTED AND REFRESHED, AND READY FOR MORE ADVENTURES. WE WALKED SEVERAL MILES OUT TO THE MAJOR HIGHWAY JUNCTION, WHERE WE FOUND A VERITABLE CROWD OF HIPPIES WAITING TO GET RIDES. ONE GUY HAD BEEN THERE FOR EIGHT HOURS. IT WAS GETTING LATE. HITCHHIKING LOOKED PRETTY HOPELESS. WE TROOPED ON BACK TO THE RAILYARD. OUR TRAIN WITH THE CULVERT PIPES WAS STILL THERE RIGHT WHERE WE'D LEFT IT. WE ASKED A YARD WORKER ABOUT TRAINS HEADED EAST. HE INFORMED US THAT THE ONE WE CAME IN ON WAS ABOUT TO PULL OUT AGAIN SHORTLY. WE CLIMBED BACK IN OUR PIPE AND SETTLED DOWN FOR ANOTHER NIGHT. BY NOW WE FELT OURSELVES TO BE OLD HANDS AT THIS BUMMING TRAINS BUSINESS.

THE TRAIN DIDN'T STOP ANYWHERE ALL THE NEXT DAY. IN THE AFTERNOON I HAD A BAD CASE OF THE RUNS AND HAD TO SHIT OFF THE END OF THE FLAT CAR WHILE HANGING ON TO THE CABLES THAT HELD THE CULVERT PIPES IN PLACE. I SAW MY DIARRHEA GO FLYING INTO THE AIR IN A LONG STREAM... A LOVELY SIGHT.

EARLY THE NEXT MORNING THE TRAIN PULLED INTO A HUGE YARD IN NORTH PLATTE, NEBRASKA. THE TWO OF US LAY LIMP INSIDE THE PIPE FEELING VERY WEAK AND LISTLESS. WE'D HAD NO FOOD OR WATER SINCE THAT RESTAURANT IN CHEYENNE. A YARD WORKER POKED HIS HEAD IN OUR PIPE AND WARNED US THAT WE'D BETTER GET OUT OF THERE FAST BECAUSE THEY WERE ABOUT TO "BUMP" THE CARS TO UNCOUPLE THEM AND WE COULD BE KILLED BY THE IMPACT. WE THANKED HIM AND TUMBLED OUT OF THERE. WE PLODDED ACROSS ROWS OF TRACKS AND CAME TO A SMALL ROAD THAT RAN ALONGSIDE THE YARD. A PICK-UP TRUCK CAME UP THE ROAD AND STOPPED BESIDE US. A HEAVY-SET CREW-CUTTED MAN IN A BROWN SUIT BARKED AT US, "HEY! DID YOU GUYS JUST GET OFF THAT TRAIN?" "YEAH," I SAID. I DIDN'T CARE ANYMORE. I WAS HALF DEAD. "GET IN THE TRUCK," HE ORDERED US. HE DROVE US TO A LITTLE POLICE STATION BELONGING TO THE RAILROAD. IT HAD JAIL CELLS AND EVERYTHING. HE WAS A DETECTIVE FOR THE UNION PACIFIC. HE SAT AT A BIG DESK POLISHING HIS BIG BROWN SHOES AND QUESTIONING US... A REAL STEREOTYPE. MY FRIEND BECAME INDIGNANT; "THE RAILROADS SHOULD BELONG TO THE PEOPLE, MAN—" THE BIG GUY CUT HIM OFF. "DON'T CALL ME MAN! I DON'T WANNA HEAR THAT BEATNIK CRAP." HE GROWLED WITH CONTEMPT. WE WERE GIVEN TWO OPTIONS; BUY TICKETS AND TAKE THE PASSENGER TRAIN OUT OF NORTH PLATTE OR SPEND THIRTY DAYS IN LOCK-UP. THE KID FROM BOSTON DIDN'T WANT TO CALL HIS PARENTS. THEY'D FLIP OUT, HE TOLD ME. I SAID I'D TRY TO GET US THE MONEY. I CALLED MY WIFE AND EXPLAINED THE SITUATION. SHE WAS PISSED AT ME FOR WALKING OUT WITHOUT EVEN SO MUCH AS A GOOD-BYE AND GOOD LUCK. I BEGGED HER FORGIVENESS AND GOT HER TO WIRE A HUNDRED DOLLARS FAST. WE BOUGHT TICKETS TO CHICAGO. WHILE WE WAITED FOR THE TRAIN THE GRUFF OLD DETECTIVE BROWSED THROUGH MY SKETCHBOOK. HE GOT A FEW CHUCKLES OUT OF IT. I ENDED UP KIND OF LIKING THE OLD BASTARD.

SO THERE WE WERE, ALL OF A SUDDEN, RIDING IN STYLE WITH A LOT OF WELL-DRESSED MIDDLE-CLASS PEOPLE IN A PASSENGER TRAIN... IT WAS STRANGE.

IN CHICAGO I GOT A CALL AT MARTY'S FROM RALPH GINZBURG... HE WAS A NEW YORK HUSTLER WHO HAD GOTTEN MILES OF PUBLICITY OUT OF HAVING BEEN BUSTED FOR PUBLISHING THIS LAVISH, EXPENSIVE, PRETENTIOUS SEX MAGAZINE CALLED EROS. EROS WAS VERY DARING FOR THOSE TIMES. RALPH MILKED THIS BUST FOR YEARS. HE HAD THIS AD SHOWING A MUG-SHOT-TYPE SET OF PHOTOS OF HIMSELF. HE WAS AN OBNOXIOUS PRESENCE IN THAT ERA. NOW HE WAS DOING A NEW MAGAZINE EQUALLY LAVISH AND PRETENTIOUS CALLED AVANT GARDE. THE CARTOON EDITOR OF CAVALIER, A RUN-OF-THE-MILL PLAYBOY IMITATION, HAD SHOWN RALPH SOME OF THE CARTOONS OF MINE THAT HE WAS RUNNING. RALPH DUG THE STUFF AND WANTED ME TO DO A LONG PIECE FOR AVANT GARDE... AS MUCH AS SEVEN PAGES IF I WANTED TO. THE PAY WAS VERY GOOD. I SET TO WORK RIGHT AWAY AND TURNED OUT SEVEN PAGES IN THREE DAYS, SITTING AT MARTY'S KITCHEN TABLE. I STILL HAD SOME MONEY LEFT, AND TOOK THE GREYHOUND TO NEW YORK.

WELL, RALPHY DIDN'T APPRECIATE AV'N'GAR COMIX. I'D DONE A NICE COLOR 'COVER' AND SIX PAGES OF CRAZY PSYCHEDELIC STRIPS. HE DIDN'T GET IT AT ALL. HE WANTED SOMETHING MORE "COHESIVE"... A "STORY LINE", A "THEME"... MAN, WHAT A SQUARE, WHAT AN ASS-HOLE, I DECIDED. HE SUGGESTED I TRY AGAIN... I SAID OKAY,

BUT I KNEW HE'D ALWAYS MAKE MY LIFE HELL TO EARN THE FANCY MONEY HE WAS PAYING...THAT'S THE KINDA GUY HE WAS. PHOOEY ON THAT. I'M EGOTISTICAL. I DON'T LIKE EDITORIAL MEDDLING IN MY WORK. THAT'S WHY I STICK WITH THE "UNDERGROUND" STILL. THE PAY IS CERTAINLY MODEST BUT YOU HAVE THAT FREEDOM. I LEARNED THIS LESSON FROM SEEING WHAT HAPPENED TO MY HERO HARVEY KURTZMAN WHEN HE GOT TANGLED UP WITH HUGH HEFNER AND THE *PLAYBOY* EMPIRE. SO I DECIDED THEN AND THERE TO HAVE NO FURTHER BUSINESS WITH MR. GINZBURG.

I TOOK THE STRIPS DOWN TO THE OFFICE OF THE LOCAL HIPPY RAG, THE *EAST VILLAGE OTHER*, WHICH PAID EXACTLY NOTHING BUT WOULD PRINT JUST ABOUT ANYTHING. I LEFT THE PILE OF ARTWORK ON THE EDITOR'S DESK, ALL EXCEPT THE NICE COLOR COVER. THE OFFICE WAS A CHAOS...HIPPIES LOUNGED ON BROKEN-DOWN COUCHES. NOBODY KNEW ANYTHING. I WENT BACK UPTOWN ON THE SUBWAY TO THE PLACE I WAS STAYING, THE APARTMENT OF MIKE THALER, THE CARTOON EDITOR OF *CAVALIER*. THALER WAS GOING OUT THAT NIGHT. I DECIDED TO TAKE SOME LSD HE'D GIVEN ME, ALONE IN HIS PLACE. NOT A SMART IDEA...ANOTHER YOUTHFUL FOLLY. OF COURSE, IT STARTED TO TURN BAD PRETTY QUICKLY. I FELT HORRIBLY ALONE AND OVERWHELMED BY THE CRUEL HARSHNESS OF NEW YORK CITY. SOON IT BEGAN TO GET REALLY FRIGHTENING. THE ROAR OF THE GIANT CITY SURROUNDED ME, CLOSING IN ON ME, MAKING MY HEAD SPIN. SIRENS WAILED IN MY BRAIN, THE SCREAMS OF THE SUFFERING, DYING MASSES OF HUMANITY GOT LOUDER AND LOUDER. IT WAS ALL LIKE SOME HOKEY IMAGE IN ONE OF THOSE FILM NOIR MOVIES OF THE LATE 'FORTIES. I WAS ABOUT TO START SCREAMING WHEN THE PHONE RANG.

A VERY FRIENDLY VOICE BROUGHT ME BACK FROM THE EDGE. IT WAS THE EDITOR OF THE *EAST VILLAGE OTHER*, WALTER BOWART, CALLING TO TELL ME HOW MUCH THEY ALL LOVED MY CARTOONS OVER THERE, WHAT A BRILLIANT TALENT I WAS AND ALL LIKE THAT. WE TALKED FOR A COUPLE OF HOURS ON THE PHONE AND I FELT INFINITELY BETTER. WALTER, I'LL ALWAYS BE GRATEFUL. GOD LOVE YA!

I RETURNED TO SAN FRANCISCO AND IMMEDIATELY WENT TO WORK ON THE FIRST ISSUE OF *ZAP COMIX*. NUMBER ONE WAS PUBLISHED IN FEBRUARY OF 1968, AND BY THE FALL OF THAT YEAR I WAS ALREADY A MINOR CULT HERO. THAT'S WHEN THINGS *REALLY* STARTED TO GO ASS-OVER-TEA KETTLE. BUT I WON'T GET INTO ALL THAT CRAP HERE. ANYWAY IT WAS AFTER ALL THE STUFF IN THIS *HEAD COMIX* BOOK WAS DONE. THIS IS STILL THE *INNOCENT* PERIOD HERE.. FAME ABRUPTLY ENDED THIS PHASE, AND MY LIFE TURNED INTO SOMETHING QUITE DIFFERENT FROM THEN ON. IT GOT VERY CONFUSING. I WAS STILL ONLY 25 YEARS OLD WHEN FAME CAME TO ME, AND THE 'SEVENTIES LAY AHEAD YET ... OY, THE 'SEVENTIES...DON'T ASK ME ABOUT *THAT* FUCKING DECADE! I STILL HAVEN'T SORTED IT OUT YET. SOME DAY I'M GONNA WRITE A BOOK! IT ALL PILED ON ME SO THICK AND FAST THERE FROM '68 ON THROUGH THE MID-'SEVENTIES....THE PRAISE, THE GLORY, THE ATTENTION..., THE PESTS! CONSTANT PESTS! THE MONEY! THE ENDLESS SQUABBLES ABOUT THE MONEY! THE BATTLE OVER THE OWNERSHIP OF "KEEP ON TRUCKIN'" THE BATTLE WITH THE I.R.S., THE BATTLE WITH THE WOMEN, NOT TO MENTION THE BATTLE OF TRYING TO GET SOME ARTWORK DONE! HEY, I SURVIVED! I'M STILL IN ONE PIECE! I'M HERE TO TELL ABOUT IT! BIG DEAL! I GOT A LOVELY WIFE AND DAUGHTER, AND I'M INTO MY WORK! I'M A LUCKY GUY.

~~~ WINTERS, CALIF.
SEPTEMBER, '87

R. Crumb's HEAD COMIX

DEFINITELY A CASE OF DERANGEMENT!

MY WIFE CRINGES IN A CORNER WHILE I STALK THE HOUSE, A RAVING LUNATIC!

I WANT MY MONEY BACK!

RIDICULOUS!

PHOOEY!

KRIPES!

NUTS! CANCEL MY RHUMBA LESSON!

FROM THE BEDROOM CLOSET I OPERATE A HUGE NETWORK OF RADIOS, SENDING OUT INCANTATIONS, CURSES, VOODOO HOODOO!

I'VE BEEN CALLED AN EVIL GENIUS BY CITIES OF ASS-HOLES... BUT I KNOW WHO THESE PEOPLE ARE! AND THEY'RE ON MY LIST!

I MAY BE NUTS BUT A SPEEDFREAK I AINT!

THE TRUTH IS, I'M ONE OF THE WORLD'S LAST GREAT MEDIEVAL THINKERS!

YOU MIGHT SAY I'M A MAD SCIENTIST, FOR MY PLANS HAVE ALL BEEN WORKED OUT QUITE METHODICALLY... LOGICALLY... BUT THE ENDS JUSTIFY THE MEANS... HEH HEH..

THIS COMIC BOOK IS PART OF THAT PLAN... BUT YOU'VE READ TOO MUCH ALREADY... I HAVE YOU RIGHT WHERE I WANT YOU...

SO, KITCHEE-KOO, YOU BASTARDS!

GO RIGHT ON TO THE NEXT PAGE!

LIFE AMONG THE CONSTIPATED

FRITZ IS A SOPHISTICATED, UP-TO-THE-MINUTE YOUNG FELINE COLLEGE STUDENT WHO LIVES IN A MODERN "SUPERCITY" OF MILLIONS OF ANIMALS... YES, NOT UNLIKE PEOPLE IN THEIR MANNERS AND MORALS....

Keep on Truckin'...

TRUCKIN' ON DOWN THE LINE...

HEY HEY HEY...

I SAID KEEP ON TRUCKIN'...

TRUCKIN' MY BLUES AWAY!

Mr. Natural meets God

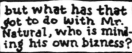

To Be Continued

Mr. Natural gets the bum's rush

Here's a couple six-second side splitters!

FRITZ THE CAT *in*
"FRITZ COMES ON STRONG"

fred the teen-age girl pigeon

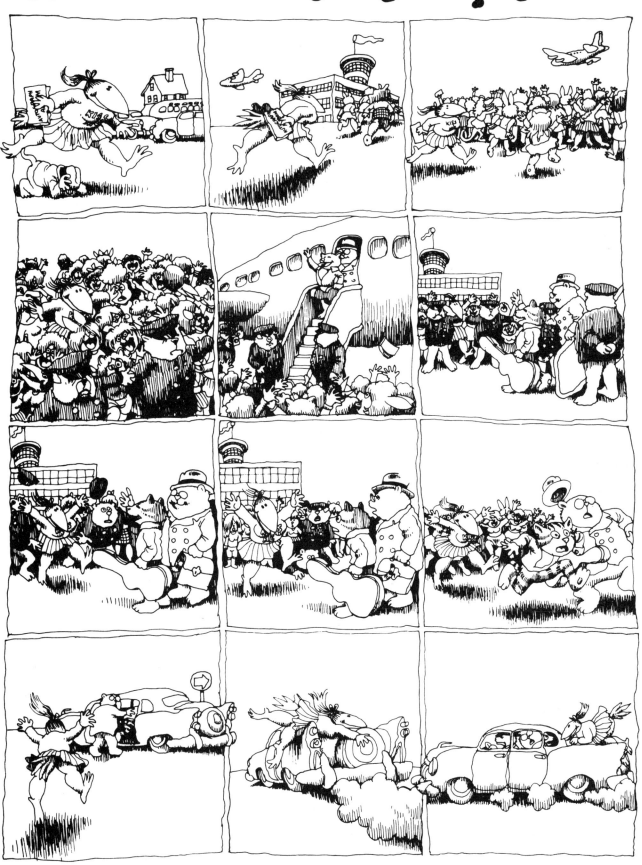

By permission of *Help!* magazine

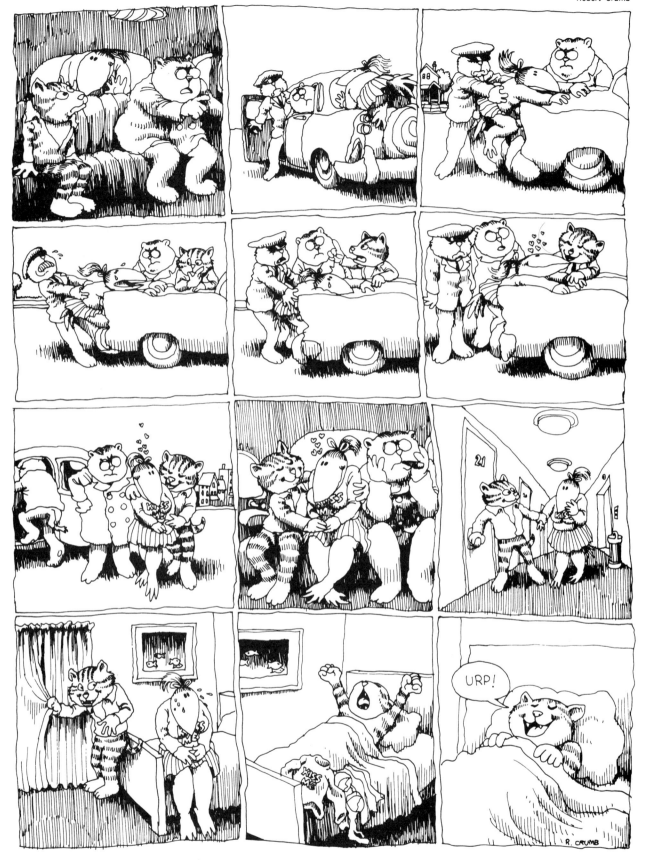

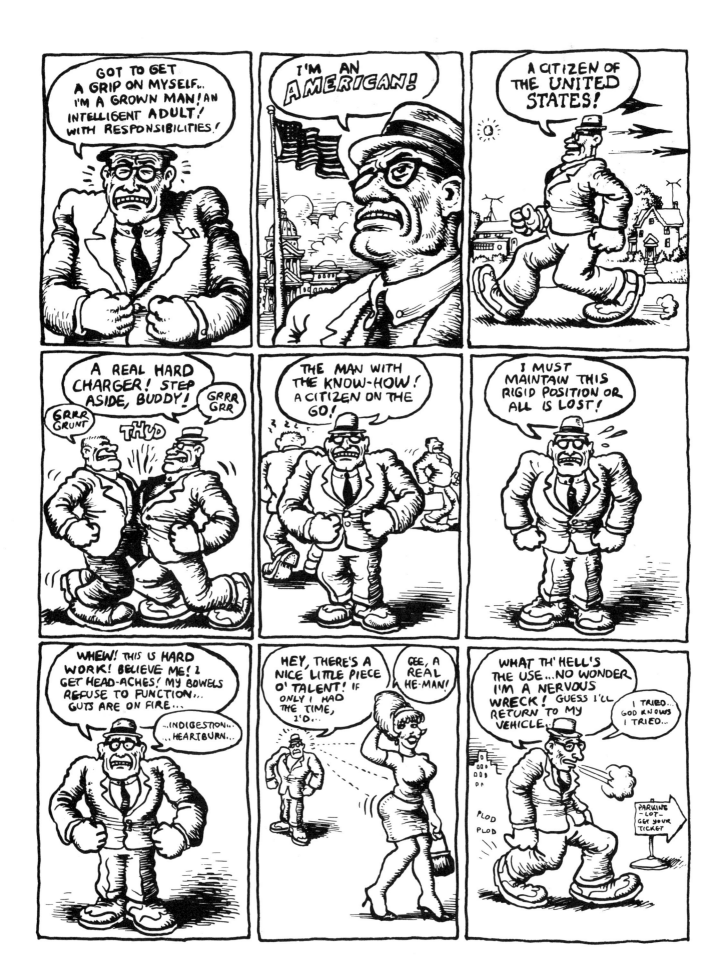

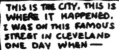

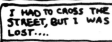

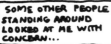

CONTINUED NEXT PAGE →

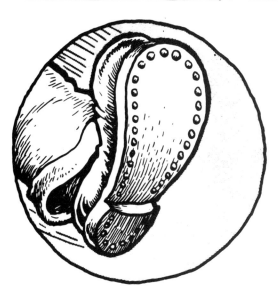

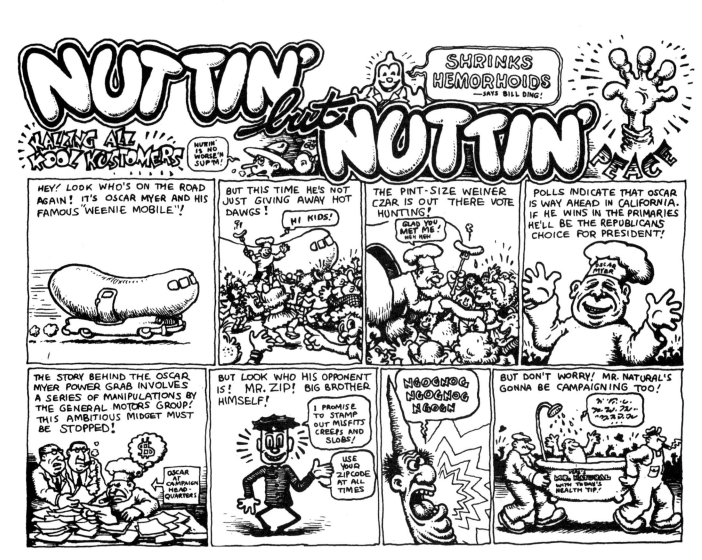

....THE END

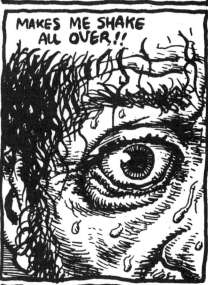

FREAK OUT FUNNIES

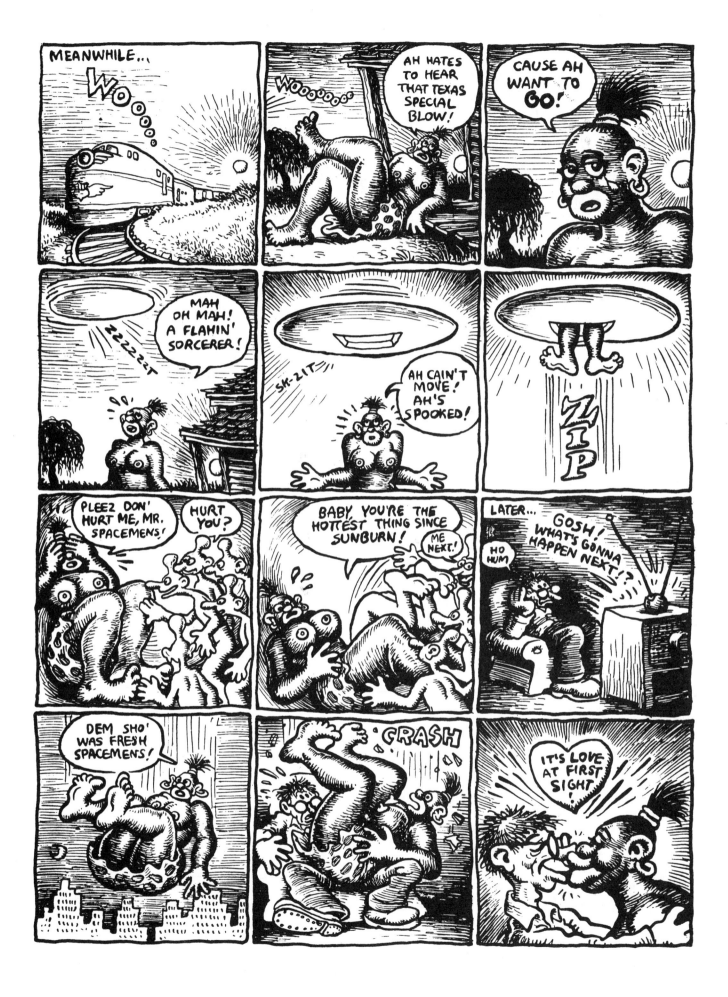

NO ONE CAN EXPLAIN IT. NO ONE KNOWS WHO'S BEHIND IT OR WHAT THE PURPOSE IS. ALL WE CAN DO IS BE GRATEFUL FOR....

MEATBALL

THE FIRST KNOWN INCIDENT TOOK PLACE IN A DIME STORE IN JERSEY CITY BACK IN 1959. A MRS. YAHOOTIE AND A MRS. KNISH WERE HAVING A TERRIBLE FIGHT.

..WHEN SUDDENLY A VOICE CRIED OUT!

MRS. YAHOOTIE GOT HIT!

MEATBALL CHANGED HER LIFE. HER NAME IS NOW A HOUSEHOLD WORD. SHE HAS MADE DOZENS OF APPEARANCES ON TV AND RADIO AND HAS BECOME AMERICA'S FAVORITE MOTHER!

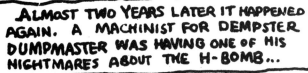

ALMOST TWO YEARS LATER IT HAPPENED AGAIN. A MACHINIST FOR DEMPSTER DUMPMASTER WAS HAVING ONE OF HIS NIGHTMARES ABOUT THE H-BOMB...

NOW THE GUY SPENDS ALL HIS TIME ANSWERING LETTERS AND PHONE CALLS FROM PEOPLE WANTING SPECIFIC DETAILS.

THEN THERE WAS THE BEATNIK WHO WAS ALWAYS HIGH...

AROUND THREE YEARS AGO, MEATBALLS BEGAN STRIKING MORE FREQUENTLY. 	PEOPLE IN ALL WALKS OF LIFE WERE GETTING HIT 	RESPECTED MEN IN HIGH PLACES WERE GETTING HIT. 
BERTRAND RUSSELL GOT HIT. 	KIM NOVAK GOT HIT ON TV IN FRONT OF MILLIONS OF VIEWERS... 	ARTICLES BEGAN TO APPEAR IN MAGAZINES. NOTED EXPERTS STATED THEIR VIEWS. 
SPEECHES WERE MADE BY MEN OF GOVERNMENT.... COMMITTEES FORMED... INVESTIGATIONS STARTED... 	THE POLICE PICKED UP SUSPICIOUS CHARACTERS BELIEVED TO BE INVOLVED IN THE MEATBALL "PLOT." 	THEN ONE SMOGGY TUESDAY IN LOS ANGELES, AROUND 12 NOON, EVERYONE IN THE DOWNTOWN AREA HEARD THE CRY... WHAT FOLLOWED IS HISTORY. 

IT RAINED MEATBALLS IN DOWNTOWN LOS ANGELES FOR ALMOST 15 MINUTES!

THOUSANDS OF PEOPLE ALL WERE HIT AT THE SAME TIME

THERE WAS RIOTING AND LOOTING AND DANCING IN THE STREETS AND A LOT OF GIGGLING!

COPS BUSTED HEADS BUT THEY COULDN'T STOP WHAT HAD HAPPENED.

SINCE "MEATBALL TUESDAY" IT APPEARS THAT THE NUMBER OF INSTANCES HAS STARTED TO TAPER OFF...

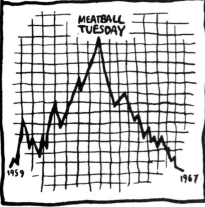

FOR MANY OF THOSE WHO HAVEN'T YET ENCOUNTERED THE MEATBALL, THE DECLINE IS A CONSTANT SOURCE OF ANXIETY AS THEY WAIT AND HOPE THAT SOME FINE DAY THEY TOO.....BUT ALAS...

MEATBALL DOESN'T WORK THAT WAY!

—THE END—